This book was given to

_____

on this day

_____

By

_____

If we seek Him, we will find Him;
and the more we seek Him,
the more we will know Him
and the more we will love Him.

Based on Matthew 7

A Year of Prayers

written and compiled by Mike Brooks
illustrated by Valerie Greeley

THOMAS NELSON PUBLISHERS
NASHVILLE

First published in the United States in 1993
by Thomas Nelson Publishers, Nelson Place at Elm Hill Pike, P.O. Box 141000
Nashville, Tennessee, USA

Design: Enid Fairhead F.C.S.D.
House Editor: Margaret McCarthy
House Designer: Hilary Edwards-Malam

Library of Congress Cataloguing in Publication Data is available.
Library of Congress Card
92–50711

ISBN 0–8407–6888–5

FOREWORD

This book includes a wide selection of prayers for all the family covering the many and varied experiences we all share. Many of the prayers are original to the author, others are well-known and a traditional part of our upbringing. All are carefully chosen and illustrated to take us through the year.

Sections such as 'Being Good, Doing Good' are written specially for the young child. Take time with your child to read the prayers thoughtfully, encouraging him or her to explore all the areas of our lives which can be shared with God. We know that we can bring to Him all our joys and sorrows, hopes and fears; for above all things, He is a God who listens when we pray.

CONTENTS

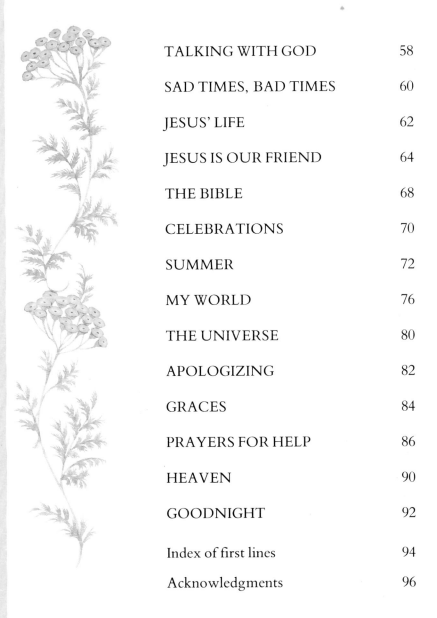

A NEW DAY

Thank you, God in heaven
For a day begun.
Thank you for the breezes,
Thank you for the sun.
For this time of gladness,
For our work and play,
Thank you, God in heaven
For another day.

Traditional

Dear Lord, thank you for a brand new day.
Thank you for all the different things I can do.
Please help me not just to do the things that make me happy,
but help me to remember others and to be kind and helpful.
Please help me today, Lord Jesus. Amen.

Thank you, dear Father, for this new day.
Help us to remember that every new day
is a gift from you, to be lived according to the rules
you have set before us in the Bible.
Help us to obey, and if we fail,
teach us that you are waiting to forgive us. Amen.

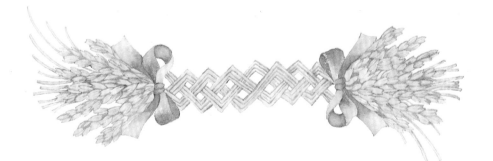

Lord, help me every day
To love you more and more,
And try to do your will
Much better than before.

R Brown-Borthwick, circa 1877 (adapted)

Hear me, Holy Father,
As to you I pray,
Asking you to keep me
Safe from harm today.

Traditional (adapted)

Autumn

Thank you God for autumn days,
With shining fields and golden sheaves
And ripening fruits and rustling leaves;
For corn and flour and new-made bread,
And golden butter quickly spread.
Thank you for the friendly cow
Who gives us milk to make us grow;
For woolly sheep and clothing warm
To keep us all from cold and harm;
For nuts and fruits and berries red,
Upon the trees and bushes spread.
Parents and children and animals and birds
Say, "Thank you very much, dear God."

Mary Osborn

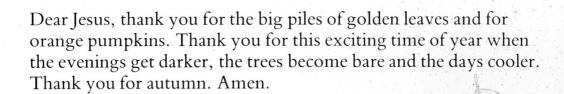

Dear Jesus, thank you for the big piles of golden leaves and for orange pumpkins. Thank you for this exciting time of year when the evenings get darker, the trees become bare and the days cooler. Thank you for autumn. Amen.

We thank you, God, for eyes to see
The beauty of the earth;
For ears to hear the words of love
And happy sounds of mirth;
For minds that find new thoughts to think,
New wonders to explore;
For health and freedom to enjoy
The good you have in store.

Jeanette Perkins Brown, 1887–1960 (adapted)

Dear God, thank you for autumn. I love this time of year. All the leaves are changing color. They fall from the trees and cover the ground like a golden brown carpet. As the days get colder we know that winter will soon be here. Please help all the wildlife as it prepares for winter, too. Amen.

Margaret McCarthy

HARVEST

Dear Jesus,

It was the harvest festival today. At school,
there was a big collection of all kinds of food:
cans and packets, fruit and vegetables.
Thank you for all this food that will go to people
who are in need.
    Some of it will travel all the way
across the world to help feed people
in countries where there is very little to eat.
    When today is over, please do not let us forget
that most of the people in the world
do not have as much to eat as we do.
Please help us to be generous and give
to those in need all the year long. Amen.

Take our gifts, O loving Jesus,
Use them in some lovely way,
For the happiness and comfort
Of the whole wide world today.

Let us be allowed to help you,
In some plan of loving care,
In some service for your kingdom,
By our offering and our prayer.

Margaret Cropper

First the seed
And then the grain;
Thank you, God
For sun and rain.

First the flour
And then the bread;
Thank you, God
That we are fed.

Thank you, God
For all your care;
Help us all
To love and share.

Lilian Cox

SCHOOL

Lord, sometimes at holiday-time we shout, "Hooray! No school today!" Sometimes we think how wonderful it would be if every day were a holiday! But there are children in other countries who would love to go to school, to learn to read, to learn to write, to learn to count.

Forgive us, Lord, for all the knowledge we take for granted. Help us to value all we learn, and bless those who pass their knowledge on to others. Amen.

Lord Jesus, when you were a boy on the earth, you went to the temple and listened to the wise men. May we follow your example. Help us to listen to our teachers in school. Help us to understand and to learn from what they say. Help us to be polite in the classroom, and not to talk when we should be listening. Amen.

Dear Jesus, I am having difficulty at school. I find it hard to do the work and I am not doing as well as many of the other children. Please help me to do my best and not to worry about it. Please let those around me understand and help me to learn.
Amen.

The end of school brings a sense of release, Lord. Classes are over for a few weeks and we can do new things and relax from our daily schedules. Thank you for what we have achieved during this year:

for new facts we have learned,
for new experiences we have shared,
for the talents of our teachers,
and for the skills of those who
run the school. Amen.

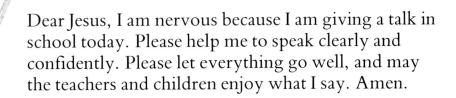

Dear Jesus, I am nervous because I am giving a talk in school today. Please help me to speak clearly and confidently. Please let everything go well, and may the teachers and children enjoy what I say. Amen.

GAMES AND HOBBIES

Did you have a hobby, Jesus?
Did you collect anything when you were a boy?
I wonder what kind of sports you played with the other children?
I wonder if your father let you make things in his woodwork shop?
Thank you for our hobbies, Lord Jesus. Amen.

Dear Lord, thank you for creating music.
Thank you for all the different
kinds of instruments
and different kinds of music.
And thank you that no matter
where they live in the world,
and no matter how rich or poor they are,
everyone has an instrument with which
they can say thank you to you – *their voice!* Amen.

Lord Jesus, sometimes when we watch
a program and we see earthquakes, bombs,
disasters, and floods, they seem to be very exciting.
But in real life, families, like my family, lose their
homes or are killed. Help me to understand this
when I watch news reports on television. Amen.

Dear Father, help me to enjoy the games I play with my friends. Help me to play fair, and to help others join in and enjoy the game. If I win, help me not to make others feel bad by showing off or by being big-headed. Teach me to be a good loser and a gracious winner. Amen.

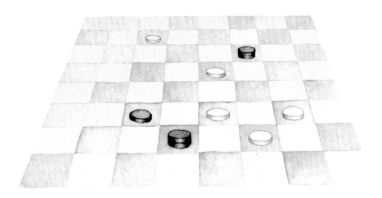

Dear Father, I know you do not like it when we cheat, or play unfairly, but I cheated in a game today. I suppose it was because I wanted to win so much. I'm sorry for cheating. Help me to enjoy playing games even when I do not win. Help me not to cheat again. Amen.

Lord Jesus, thank you for all the sports we can play, like football and baseball, basketball and soccer. And thank you for the places we have to play, for fields and parks and playgrounds. Keep us safe as we play. Amen.

Advent and Christmas

Dear Jesus, Advent is the time of year we know as the Christmas season. Throughout Advent we think about when you came into the world as a baby, born in a stable. It is also a time when people have parties and dress up and exchange presents and cards. Help us, dear Jesus, not to leave you out. And help us to leave anything out of Christmas that would make us forget about you. Amen.

In those days the Emperor ordered a census to be taken throughout the Roman Empire, and everyone was required to return to his hometown to be registered. So Joseph went from Nazareth in Galilee to a town called Bethlehem, in Judea. He went there with Mary. Mary was pregnant, and while they were in Bethlehem, the time came for her to have her baby. But there was no room for them to stay at the inn, so she gave birth to her first son in the nearby stable. She wrapped Him in strips of cloth and laid Him in a manger.

Based on Luke 2

Some shepherds were spending the night in the fields nearby, taking care of their sheep. An angel of the Lord appeared to them, and the glory of the Lord shone over them. They were terribly afraid, but the angel said to them, "Do not be afraid! I am here with good news for you, which will bring great joy to all the people. This very day your Savior was born – Christ the Lord! And this will prove it to you: you will find a baby wrapped in strips of cloth and lying in a manger." Suddenly, a great army of heaven's angels also appeared, singing this praise to God: "Glory to God in the highest heaven, and peace on earth to those with whom He is pleased!"

Based on Luke 2

Lord Jesus, I would hate it if my friends were so busy enjoying themselves and opening presents of their own on my birthday, that they forget all about me. Please help me not to do that to you. Amen.

Zinnia Bryan

Thank you, Lord Jesus, for our nativity play. Thank you for all those who have helped us to make our costumes, and who have helped to make the stage look so nice. Please help us to play our parts well, and let everyone enjoy it. Amen.

Wind through the olive trees
Softly did blow
Round little Bethlehem,
Long, long ago.

Sheep on the hillside lay
Whiter than snow
Shepherds were watching them,
Long, long ago.

Then from the happy sky
Angels bent low
Singing their songs of joy,
Long, long ago.

For in a manger bed
Cradled, we know,
Christ came to Bethlehem,
Long, long ago.

Thank you, Heavenly Father!
Amen.

Anon

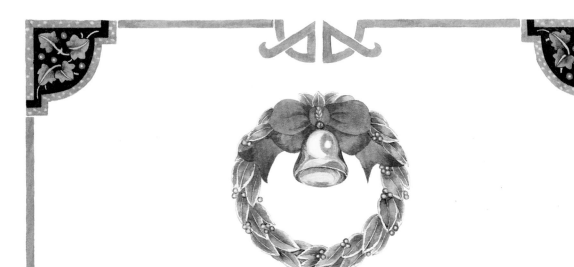

Dear Jesus, how different Christmas was for you. You did not have presents or a party or lots of food or toys or games. Instead you were laid in a small and smelly stable. It mustn't have been very nice. Please help us to remember that Christmas is not about having lots of presents but about trusting in you. Amen.

Dear Jesus, thank you for this time of year when we think about your birth in a manger, in a stable in Bethlehem, many years ago. I am thankful that you are still alive today, listening to our prayers. Amen.

THE NEW YEAR

Lord, let this New Year be a new beginning for all your children, everywhere. Please guide us in finding new ways of helping each other, at home, at school; with friends and family. Let us not quarrel over little things but have the courage to speak up and defend what we know is right. Let us not take your world for granted, but be aware of its beauty. Let us not forget those who face trouble and hardship this year. Let us trust that your love will be with us all, forever. Amen.

Margaret McCarthy

Dear Jesus, when it is New Year, some people make promises to do things differently. They call it making New Year's resolutions. I want to make one too, Lord Jesus. I want to stop doing bad things and ask you to be my friend – every day. Please help me to keep to my New Year's resolution. Amen.

Dear Jesus, New Year can be a fun time – with parties and music and fun – but it is also the end of the holiday season. Christmas is over and school will be beginning again soon. There are rooms to be cleaned and chores to be done. But even though there are no more presents, thank you that every day can be a special day because you are always with us. Amen.

It is a New Year! One year has gone by, and another is just beginning. I wonder what will happen during the year ahead. It can be exciting to think of all that time ahead of us. Please make it a good year, Lord Jesus, for all my family. Amen.

Epiphany

Soon after Jesus' birth, some wise men came from the east to Jerusalem and asked, "Where will the baby be born who will be the King of the Jews? We saw His star when it came up in the east, and we have come to worship Him." They were told that Jesus was to be born in Bethlehem, and so they left, and on their way they saw the star again. They were overjoyed to see it. It went ahead of them until it stopped over the place where the child was. They went into the house, and when they saw the child with His mother Mary, they knelt down and worshiped Him. They brought out their gifts of gold, frankincense and myrrh, and presented them to Him. Then they went back to their own country.

Based on Matthew 2

 Dear Jesus, at this time of the year, we remember the wise men and the miles and miles they journeyed just so they could see you in the stable. Please may we be like the wise men, and always want to be with you. Amen.

Dear Jesus, when the wise men saw you in the manger you were so small and weak – and yet you were still the King and the wise men worshiped you. How wonderful you are! How majestic! Grown up men bowed down before you and loved you. May we be like the wise men. Amen.

Dear Jesus, you were once a tiny baby. You slept and cried and needed feeding, and Joseph and Mary looked after you. Thank you, Lord Jesus, that you know what being a child is like. Thank you, Lord Jesus, for the grownups who look after me. Amen.

Dear Lord, what an unusual and beautiful star it must have been to make the wise men follow it all the way to Bethlehem. Then when they found you they were not disappointed – because you were even more beautiful. Thank you for coming into this world to help us, Lord Jesus. Thank you that you are still with us. Amen.

PRAISE AND WORSHIP

We praise God for things we see,
The growing flower, the waving tree,
Our mother's face, the bright blue sky,
Where birds and clouds go floating by;
   Praise to God for seeing.

We praise God for things we hear,
The voices of our playmates dear,
The merry bells, the songs of birds,
Stories and tunes and kindly words;
   Praise to God for hearing. Amen.

Maria Matilda Penstone

Dear God, thank you for being so great!
Thank you because you know everything,
and can do anything.
Thank you for being everywhere.
Thank you for being there to listen.
Thank you for being always good, kind and fair.
Thank you because even though you are so important,
you still care for little people like me. Amen.

God is in heaven.
He does care,
He is good to me.
Yes, all I have, and all I love,
It's God that gives it to me.

Thank you, God!

Anne Gilbert, 1782–1866 (adapted)

We praise the Lord for all the seasons,
We praise Him for the gentle spring,
We praise the Lord for glorious summer,
Birds and beasts and everything.
We praise the Lord, who sends the harvest,
We praise Him for the winter snows,
Praise the Lord all you who love Him,
Praise Him, for all things He knows. Amen.

Mary Anderson

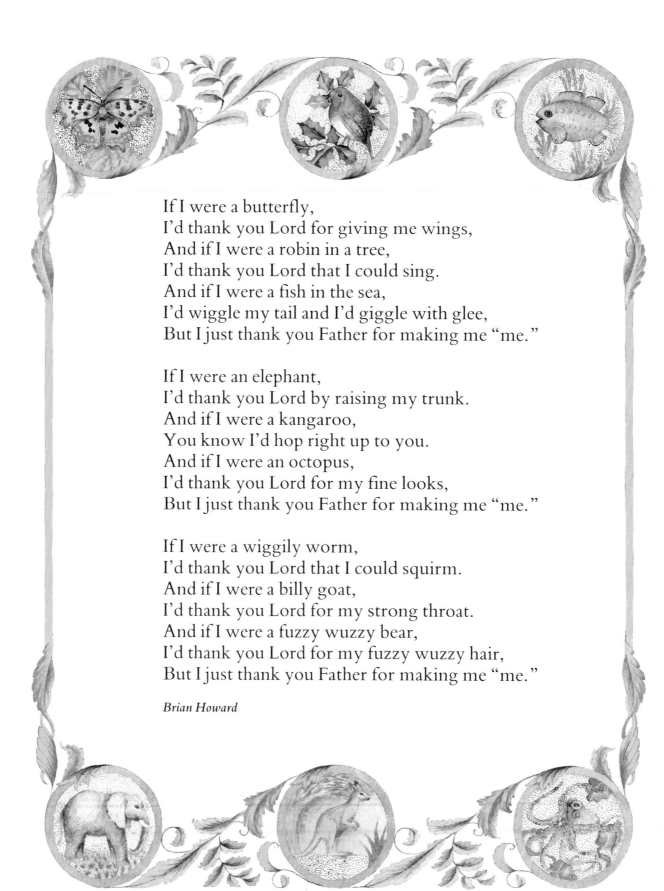

If I were a butterfly,
I'd thank you Lord for giving me wings,
And if I were a robin in a tree,
I'd thank you Lord that I could sing.
And if I were a fish in the sea,
I'd wiggle my tail and I'd giggle with glee,
But I just thank you Father for making me "me."

If I were an elephant,
I'd thank you Lord by raising my trunk.
And if I were a kangaroo,
You know I'd hop right up to you.
And if I were an octopus,
I'd thank you Lord for my fine looks,
But I just thank you Father for making me "me."

If I were a wiggily worm,
I'd thank you Lord that I could squirm.
And if I were a billy goat,
I'd thank you Lord for my strong throat.
And if I were a fuzzy wuzzy bear,
I'd thank you Lord for my fuzzy wuzzy hair,
But I just thank you Father for making me "me."

Brian Howard

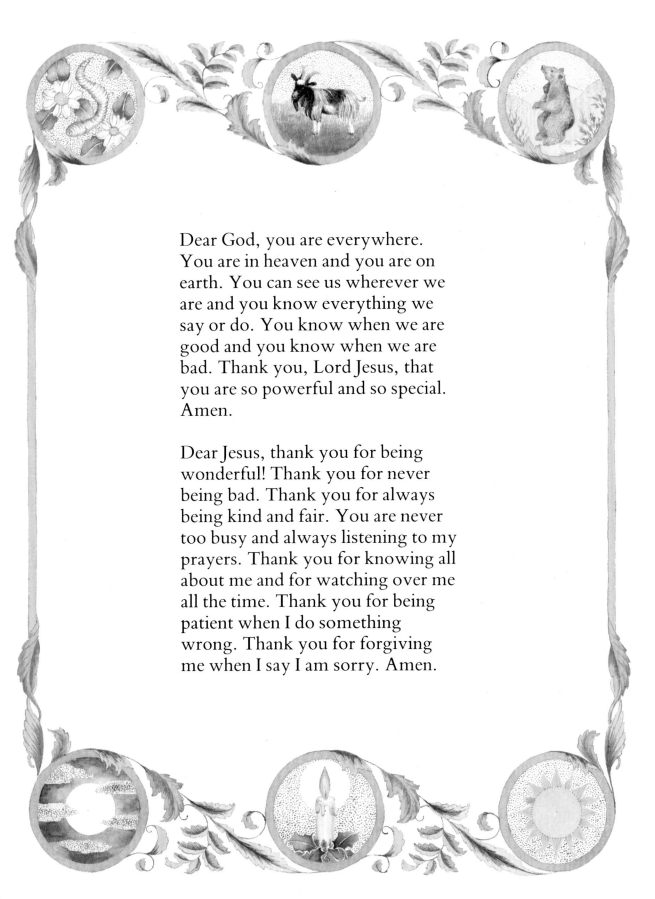

Dear God, you are everywhere. You are in heaven and you are on earth. You can see us wherever we are and you know everything we say or do. You know when we are good and you know when we are bad. Thank you, Lord Jesus, that you are so powerful and so special. Amen.

Dear Jesus, thank you for being wonderful! Thank you for never being bad. Thank you for always being kind and fair. You are never too busy and always listening to my prayers. Thank you for knowing all about me and for watching over me all the time. Thank you for being patient when I do something wrong. Thank you for forgiving me when I say I am sorry. Amen.

Winter

We thank you, loving Father God
For things which warm us so;
For glowing fires and woolly gloves
Which make cold fingers glow;
For winter clothes and games to play
When we can skip and run . . .
And thank you for our cozy beds
When winter's day is done. Amen.

Hilda Rostron

What a day! It's raining so hard it's almost like a flood,
and the trees look like they might blow over in the wind!
It's fun being inside when it's cold and stormy outside.
Thank you for my warm, dry house.
Please keep all the cars and drivers safe on the roads,
and please look after those who are living outside
in the cold. Amen.

Dear God, we wake in the morning to see a
white world: hooray! With boots and scarves
and joyous shouts, we're out! The snow's so
soft, so cold to taste! With grown-up help, and
laughs and shouts, we shape a man, with eyes
of stones, and a carrot nose. We drag a sled to
the nearest slope: we slide and roll, and blink
back tears in the icy cold. Father God, what fun
we have in the snow! Thank you! Help us to
remember the people for whom snow makes
life more difficult, and show us how we can
help them. Amen.

Dear Lord, winter can be a fun time of the year, when we wear
our warm clothes and have hot drinks. But some people,
especially old people, can get very ill in the wintertime. Please
help people remember to look after the old people. Amen.

PEOPLE WE MEET

Lord, we thank you that when you filled the world with people, you did not make us all alike! Instead you made a world where people –

    live in different countries,
    have skins of different colors,
    speak many different languages,
    live with different customs.

Lord, sometimes we are afraid of people who are different from ourselves, because we do not understand them.

Help us and all our children to see that you are a God big enough to hold all the differences of the world within your loving arms. Amen.

    Dear Jesus, thank you that we are all different,
    and that we each have different skills and abilities.
    No one can say, "I am more special than you are,"
    because we are all equally special in your eyes. Amen.

Forgive me, dear Jesus, because sometimes I look at the clothes others are wearing and I am jealous. I think, "I must have clothes like that!" or sometimes I look down on them and think, "I'm glad I don't wear clothes like that!" Please help me to remember that it is not what people look like on the outside, but what they are like on the inside that really matters. Amen.

Lord, often we say, "I'm hungry!" and pick up a cookie, or a packet of chips, or some sweets.
Help us to understand what it feels like to be really hungry and to have nothing to eat.
We pray for those who try to help hungry people, by sharing their skills, knowledge and tools.
Help us to share what we have, so that everyone may have food to eat. Amen.

Lord God, when you made us, you made others too. Help us to get along with the people around us.

Forgive us when we are afraid of other people
because they seem different from us.
Forgive us when we are jealous of other people
because they seem to be happier or more successful than us.
Forgive us when we look down on other people
because we feel that we are better than they are.

Help us to love others as you love us, and to remember that other people are your children, too. Amen.

Jesus sat in the temple watching as the people came and put money in the temple treasury. The rich people were putting a lot of money in the money box. Then, a poor woman came along and put just two small coins in the treasury. Jesus was more pleased with what the poor lady had given than all the money the rich people had given. He called His disciples over to tell them why. "I tell you, this poor woman put more in the offering box than all the others. The others put in what they had to spare out of their riches; but she, poor as she is, put in all she had – she gave all she had to live on."

Based on Mark 12

Dear Heavenly Father, thank you that even though there are many people all over the world in different countries, you see us all, and watch over us. Thank you, dear God, that even though we cannot see you, you can see us. Amen.

Jesus, you knew that you needed friends.
You needed someone to talk to,
someone to comfort you
and care for you.
So you chose twelve men
and asked them to go with you
wherever you went.
Like true friends, they went with you.
Jesus, we need friends, too.
Please help us to make friends,
and help us to be good friends, too. Amen.

YOU AND ME

Dear Jesus, thank you for my body.
I notice that there are many
different kinds of bodies:
fat ones, thin ones, tall ones, short ones,
and all shapes in between!
Thank you that you love all bodies just the same.
Amen.

Dear Jesus, you made people a long time ago
at the beginning of the world. You made people
different from the animals. You made us to look
after the planet and to look after each other.
Please help us live like you want us to.
Amen.

Lord Jesus, it is difficult to know what it must be like to be
blind, because I can see; and it is hard for me to understand
what it must be like to be deaf, because I can hear; and it is
hard to imagine what it must be like to be crippled, because
I can walk and run. Thank you Lord Jesus, for eyes and ears,
and legs and feet. Amen.

O, God, bless and help all those who have to face life with
    some handicap.
Those who limp and are crippled, who cannot run and jump
    and play the games which other people play;

Those who are blind and who cannot see the light of the sun
    or the faces of their friends;

Those who are deaf, who cannot hear the voices of their
    friends, who cannot listen to music or the singing of the birds;

Those who find learning difficult, and for whom it is a constant
    struggle to keep up with the class. Amen.

William Barclay

My tongue can taste all sorts of things.
All kinds of things! So many things!
My nose can smell all sorts of things.
I thank you, Heavenly Father.

My ears can hear all sorts of things.
All kinds of things! So many things!
My eyes can see so many things.
I thank you, Heavenly Father.

My hands can touch all sorts of things.
All kinds of things! So many things!
And I can do so many things!
I thank you, Heavenly Father. Amen.

Marjorie Newman

ANIMALS AND PETS

Animals in zoos, in films, in books;
hundreds, thousands, with different looks:
the monkey and the kangaroo,
the eagle and the cockatoo;
the tall giraffe, the crawling snail,
the tiny mouse, the giant whale;
the bear, the emu and the gnat,
the crab, the donkey and the bat.
Thank you for them, large and small,
thank you, God, who made them all.

Geoffrey Marshall-Taylor

Dear Jesus, I have the best dog in the world. Whenever I come
home he is always pleased to see me. On weekends he comes into
my room and jumps on my bed to wake me up. In the evenings
we sit and watch TV together. I'm glad I have a pet, Lord.
Help me remember always to show him kindness. Amen.

Thank you, Lord Jesus, for guide dogs.
They are so useful, they are both a help
and companion to those who cannot see.
May there never be a shortage
of good guide dogs. Amen.

Thank you for the birds that I see
flying about me every day.
Thank you for the many different kinds.
Thank you for our bird feeder.
Please help us to look after
the birds you have made. Amen.

Dear God,
Please look after my kitten
when she wanders out to play.
The garden can be very big
To a kitten so small and gray.
I wonder what she thinks of grass,
and earth and sky so blue?
She knows I love her very much
And I know you love her, too.
Amen.

Winifred Huckvale

WHERE I LIVE

Dear Lord, when the winter winds howl round the house, and freezing rain beats on the windows, we're glad to be indoors. When big trees creak and groan, and young trees bend low, we shiver and are glad to be indoors.

Great Father God, we thank you for our homes.
We thank you for our families
who comfort us and make us feel safe.
We think of people who have no homes:
may they find shelter from the storm. Amen.

Thank you Jesus for my house, and for the people who built it. Thank you for my bedroom, Lord Jesus. Thank you for a place where I can put my pictures up on the wall, and keep all my books and games, clothes and things. Thank you for a place I can go to when I want to be on my own, and thank you for my warm bed. Amen.

God, our Father, please help all the people in the world
who have no real homes to live in;
who have to leave their homes, families and friends;
who have to live in tents or shelters.
May they soon have new homes, and friends who care
about them. Amen.

Lord Jesus, you lived at Nazareth in a house with a flat roof;
and listened to the stories your mother, Mary, told you.
You watched Joseph working in his carpenter's shop; and
you played with your brothers and sisters.
Lord Jesus, we are glad you had a home and family, as we do.
Help us to remember that you are always with us.

Home is the place we come to when we are tired
and want to rest, when we have some good news to share,
when we are sad and alone.
Home is the place where the people who love us are always
glad to see us. Thank you, God, for our homes and families.
Amen.

THE WORK WE DO

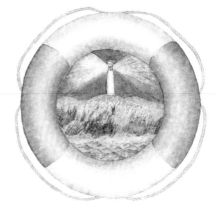

Dear Jesus, thank you for all the men and women who risk their lives to rescue us when we are in danger. They sail lifeboats and fly helicopters and make dangerous journeys to try and make people safe. Please help them to do their jobs. Amen.

Dear Jesus, today I saw a fire engine zooming down the road with its lights flashing and its siren wailing. Thank you for the brave men and women who risk their lives to keep us safe from fire. Amen.

Thank you, dear Jesus, for hospitals,
and for the doctors and nurses who work there.
Thank you for the skill and knowledge
they use to help keep us healthy. Amen.

Dear Jesus, thank you for the postal workers, the police, and the fire departments who keep working even when it is very cold. Please keep them safe on the icy roads and pavements. Also, please help us to remember to visit old people who cannot leave their homes. Amen.

Lord Jesus, I pray for the President, for the men and women who work in the Congress, and for leaders and rulers, and kings and queens all over the world.

Please give them wisdom and understanding so that they can make good decisions for the people they serve, so there is no shortage of food or clothing, and so that countries can be on friendly terms without having wars. Please help these leaders to be honest and to care for all people. Amen.

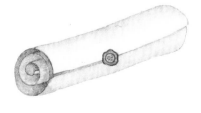

MY FAMILY

Mothers and fathers are the people who love us and
look after us; who understand when we say "sorry";
and play with us and tell us stories; who hold our hands
when we are afraid and make us smile when we are sad.
Thank you, Lord, for our mothers and fathers. Amen.

Thank you for my grandpa and grandma, dear Jesus.
Thank you that they are always thrilled to see me,
and like to give me presents.
I love it when they tell me stories of things they used to do
when they were young.
Help me to look after my grandparents. Amen.

Thank you for our new baby, Lord Jesus. He (she) is so small and helpless. He (she) needs a lot of looking after and a lot of attention. Please help me to join in helping him (her), and not to be jealous of all the attention he (she) gets, because I know I was a baby once, and I, too, needed all that help. Amen.

Help me to make my family a happy one, Lord Jesus. May I always be helpful and considerate, and not selfish, always wanting my own way. May I always remember to clean up after myself, and not leave that job for others. Amen.

Lord, we are glad we have brothers and sisters. We can play together, and help each other. When we say hurtful things, help us to say we are "sorry." When we disagree, help us to be friends. When we want to keep things all to ourselves, help us to share. Amen.

Spring

Dear Jesus, thank you for spring. Thank you for all the changes that are taking place – buds are growing on trees, new flowers are blossoming and there are different colors all around.

When everything is changing all around us, may we remember that you are always the same, Lord Jesus. You are always kind and true. Amen.

Spring is here! Thank you, God, that the days are getting warmer and the evenings are getting brighter. Thank you for the color that comes into the world at springtime. Amen.

Spring is a time for new life. We see lambs in the fields and buds begin to appear on the trees. The first flowers push their way through the soil, and all around us new life is blossoming. Thank you, God, for this season. Amen.

Lent and Easter

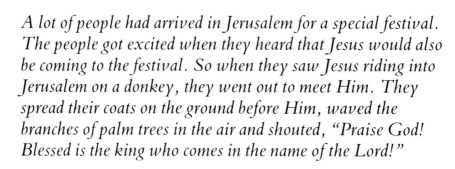

A lot of people had arrived in Jerusalem for a special festival. The people got excited when they heard that Jesus would also be coming to the festival. So when they saw Jesus riding into Jerusalem on a donkey, they went out to meet Him. They spread their coats on the ground before Him, waved the branches of palm trees in the air and shouted, "Praise God! Blessed is the king who comes in the name of the Lord!"

Based on John 12

Lord Jesus, you were tempted in the wilderness to turn away from God and do what was wrong. And yet you resisted. Instead, you looked to heaven for help and you did what was right. Thank you, Lord Jesus, that when we are your children, you will help us to do what is right. Amen.

The soldiers led Jesus away. A large crowd of people followed Him; among them were some women who were weeping and wailing. Eventually they reached the place called 'The Skull,' and there they crucified Jesus. At midday, the whole country became dark. The darkness remained for three hours until with a loud cry, "It is finished . . ." Jesus bowed His head and died.

When the army officer standing in front of the cross saw how Jesus died, he said, "Surely this man was the Son of God."

Based on Mark 15; John 19

Dear Jesus, I have been thinking a lot about Easter. Why did you let evil men put you on a cross to die when you had done nothing wrong? Even though it is hard to understand, Lord Jesus, I thank you because I know that you died for people like me, who say and do things that you don't like. Amen.

Dear Jesus, thank you that you did
not die. They tried to kill you on
the cross, but you rose from the
dead on Easter day – and now you
are alive forevermore. Amen.

Dear Jesus, I am sad when I think
about what they did to you.
Who were they, Jesus? They laughed
at you. They did not want to know
you. They did not want to hear
anything about you. They were a
bit like people today. They were
a bit like I am sometimes. I am sorry,
dear Jesus, for sometimes being like
those cruel men. Amen.

Dear Jesus, when do you love us?
You love us when we say we are
sorry for the bad things we do.
You love us when we remember that
saying we are sorry means wanting to be good instead.
Please help us to say sorry,
Lord Jesus. Amen.

Jesus' body was taken down from the cross, wrapped in a clean linen cloth and placed in a new tomb cut out of rock. A big stone was rolled in front of the tomb and a guard placed by the entrance. On the first day of the next week, very early in the morning, some women went to visit the tomb. But when they arrived, they found the stone had been rolled away from the tomb and, when they entered, they did not find the body of the Lord Jesus. Just then, two angels appeared to them and said, "Why are you looking for the living in here? Jesus has risen! He is alive!"

Based on Matthew 28

Dear Jesus,
thank you because you
are alive forevermore
and you will never die.
Thank you that we can live
forever too, if we believe
in you. Amen.

THANK YOU, GOD

Dear God, you know all about me; you know how
I feel, when I'm happy or sad; you know what I say,
when I'm kind or rude; you know what I do,
when I'm good or bad.
Dear God, thank you for knowing all about me
and still loving me. Amen.

Geoffrey Marshall-Taylor

Thanks for the rabbit
that hops and jumps.
And thanks for the camel
that has two humps.
Thank you for the animals
and games we play,
And thank you for the people
who help me each day. Amen.

Tony Davies, age 12

Thank you for my clothes
And for the food I eat
Thank you for my house
And the bed in which I sleep.

For friends and grass and trees
We thank you, Lord above.
For smiling flowers and earth,
And sunny skies above.

We know your tender love.
We thank you for your care,
For light, and fields, and flowers,
And all things everywhere. Amen.

Anon

Dear Jesus, thank you for all that you have given me. Thank you for all the things I enjoy. Thank you for friends and family, and cakes and toys and games. Amen.

BEING GOOD, DOING GOOD

Lord Jesus,
you told us to love one another.
     Please help us to do this.
Show us how to be friends
     with anyone who is lonely.
Show us how to talk
     to anyone who is unhappy.
Show us how to smile
     and cheer someone up.
Please help us, Lord. Amen.

Dear Jesus, you were always good.
You never said anything cruel or
unkind or rude. You never stole or
were mean to people. I am sorry
when I do things that are wrong.
Please help me to be like you.
Amen.

Lord Jesus, I don't want to be jealous because it is not a nice feeling. Sometimes I think about people who can do things which I cannot do, or who have things which I do not have, and I feel jealous of them. Please help me to be happy with what I can do and with what I have got. Amen.

Lord of the loving heart,
May mine be loving, too.
Lord of the gentle hands,
May mine be gentle, too.
Lord of the willing feet,
May mine be willing, too.
So may I grow more like to you
In all I say and do. Amen.

Church Missionary Society

Dear Jesus, it is an awful feeling when my friends want me to do something which I know is bad. I am scared they will stop being my friends if I don't join in. Help me to understand that it is always better to do what is right, even if it means losing friends. Amen.

Dear God, thank you for giving us the Bible.
Thank you because it shows us how to live in
the best way. Please help us to read it and do
as it says. Amen.

Dear Lord, please help me to remember poor people.
Some children do not have toys or candy.
Please help me to share what I have with them. Amen.

Dear Jesus, when I am at school I notice there are some
children who do not have anyone to talk to. I know it isn't nice
because I do not like it when I have no one to talk to. Please
help me to notice children who seem to be lonely, help me to
be friendly to them and to let them join in with what I am
doing. Amen.

Dear Jesus, sometimes it is very
clear what is a good thing and
what is a bad thing to do.
But sometimes I am not sure.
Please give me understanding
so that I can do the things which
are pleasing to you. Amen.

Dear Lord, words are so important.
The words we choose to use can make others
feel happy or sad. May our words always be kind
and helpful words, and never cruel or hurtful,
because this is the way you spoke, Lord Jesus. Amen.

TALKING WITH GOD

If you feel frightened – talk to Jesus.
If you feel happy – talk to Jesus.
If you are scared – talk to Jesus.
If you have been bad – talk to Jesus.
If you feel lonely – talk to Jesus.
If you are excited – talk to Jesus.

Dear Jesus, sometimes
when we talk to people
they do not listen.
Thank you for always
being there to listen.
Thank you that
whoever we are, we can
always talk to you.
Amen.

Thank you for always listening
No matter what I say.
Thank you for understanding
All the words I pray.
Amen.

Dear Jesus, thank you that there are so many things to pray about. We can thank you for our family and friends. We can ask you for help. We can ask you to make us good. We can say we are sorry. Or we can just think about you. Thank you for prayers. Amen.

Lord, teach me what I need,
And teach me how to pray,
And do not let me talk to you
And not mean what I say.

John Burton, 1803–1877 (adapted)

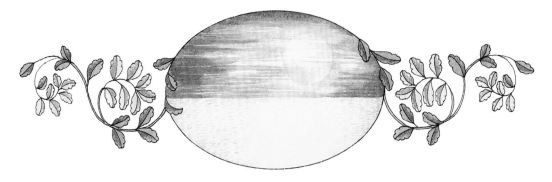

Dear Lord, when you were on the earth you found time to pray. Sometimes I find it difficult to pray.
There are days when I seem too busy or tired.
Did you ever feel like that? Help me to make time for prayer, and if, sometimes, it seems you do not answer, help me to know that you are listening and will answer in the way that is best for me. Help me, when I am doubting, to know that you are there.

Nancy Martin

SAD TIMES, BAD TIMES

Lord Jesus, you know what it is like to be sad and worried;
   please help us when we are troubled.
When we are nervous, give us courage to face our troubles,
   and to face whatever scares us.
When we are sad we are comforted,
   knowing you are there.
Help us to bring all our worries to you,
   because you understand. Amen.

Heavenly Father, please remember those who have very little
to eat, very few clothes to wear, and nowhere to sleep at night.
Some of them live in this country, some of them live overseas.
Please help us to take care of the homeless everywhere. Amen.

Dear Jesus, I am not feeling well. Please help me to get better soon. Thank you for the people who are looking after me. Please help me to remember to say "thank you." Amen.

Lord God, Lord of the world,
    sometimes it is hard for us to understand why
    nations go to war to fight and kill.
Perhaps, sometimes, we do it for money;
    sometimes to stand up for what we believe is right;
    sometimes to make ourselves seem more important;
    sometimes to protect others.
Lord of the world,
    forgive us for the selfishness which causes war.
    Help us to find ways of understanding one another
    and settling our differences without taking the lives
    which you have given to us. Amen.

JESUS' LIFE

Dear Jesus, thank you for your life. When you were on earth you showed kindness to people whenever you could; you listened when they were sad and you offered hope when they were very worried. Help me to follow your example every day. Amen.

Dear Jesus, when you were on the earth, things were very different. There were no cars or light bulbs or televisions. But hundreds of years later, the same white moon comes out at night and the same bright sun shines in the day. You are still the same as well, Lord Jesus. Thank you that you do not stop loving us. Amen.

Dear Lord, thank you for all the things you did when you were on earth. Thank you that Matthew, Mark, Luke and John all wrote about you in the Bible. Thank you for all the miracles you did, for the people you healed and for all the ways you helped people. Thank you, Lord Jesus, for coming down from Heaven. Amen.

Some people brought children to Jesus for Him to place His hands on them and pray for them. The disciples scolded the people. But Jesus said, "Let the children come to me and do not stop them, because the kingdom of heaven belongs to such as these."

Based on Matthew 19

JESUS IS OUR FRIEND

Dear Jesus, thank you that you are a better friend than even my friends at school. You never tell lies or call people names. Thank you dear Jesus, for being the best friend anyone can have. I'm sorry that I let you down by doing things that I shouldn't. Amen.

Dear God, some people find it hard to believe in you because they cannot see you. They do not know what you look like and they do not know what you do. Please teach them what you are like Jesus. Amen.

Dear Jesus, how can I be a friend of yours?
By believing in you and being a friend to
others. Lord Jesus, please help me to be
your friend. Amen.

Dear Jesus, thank you for all the promises you
made in the Bible. Thank you for saying that if
we call on you, you will not ignore us and you
will never give up on us. Thank you for caring
for us. Amen.

Dear Jesus, why is it that some people
don't want to know anything about you?
Please show them that you are kind and
loving. Show them that you want to be
their friend, even if they think they don't
want to be your friend. Amen.

Lord Jesus, sweet Jesus.
In my life may I make this my one true goal:
To know you. Amen.

Jesus, friend of little children,
Be a friend to me;
Take my hand and ever keep me
Close to thee.

Never leave me, nor forsake me,
Ever be my friend;
For I need you from life's beginning
To its end.

Walter John Mathams, 1853–1931 (adapted)

Dear Jesus, the Bible says you are like a door
because you are the way into a new kind of life
– a life where we can be your friends.
Dear Jesus, I want to be on the other side of that
door – I want to live the life of
a friend of Jesus. Amen.

Saviour, teach me, day by day,
Love's sweet lesson to obey;
Sweeter lesson cannot be,
Loving Him who first loved me.

Jane Eliza Leeson, 1809–1881

Dear Jesus, what is a friend? A friend is someone
who is always there to share happy times and bad
times and who is always ready to listen. Help me
to be a good friend and to share my feelings with
the people I love and also with you. Amen.

Thank you, Jesus, that wherever I go,
you are always there. Even when I am on my own,
you are always beside me. Thank you for wanting
to be my friend, dear Jesus.
Please help me to be a friend to others,
especially to those who are lonely. Amen.

THE BIBLE

Dear Jesus, thank you for the Bible, and for the important message it contains. Thank you for this book because without it we would not know about you. When we read the Bible, help us to understand what it means. Amen.

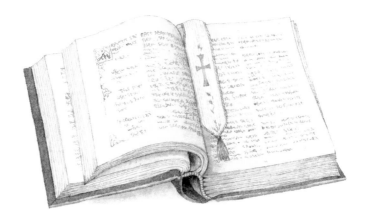

God our Father, we thank you that the Bible is not just one book but a whole library.
We thank you for its record of history, its life-stories of great people, its poetry, songs and prayers, its exciting travel tales, its letters and wise sayings.
In the Bible you have given us something for everyone to read and enjoy. Help us to read widely from its many books and so learn more about you, about the world, and about other people. Amen.

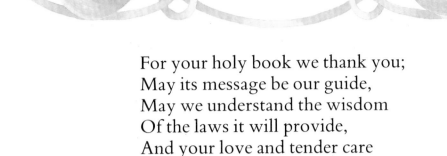

For your holy book we thank you;
May its message be our guide,
May we understand the wisdom
Of the laws it will provide,
And your love and tender care
For your people everywhere. Amen.

Ruth Carter (adapted)

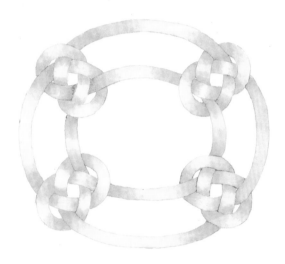

The Bible is a treasure chest of many small books. There are poems and prayers, history and stories. It starts when God made the world, and it tells us the adventures of the Jewish people.

The Bible also tells us about the life of Jesus. It tells us all we need to know about Jesus and God. It teaches us that Jesus is God, and shows us how much He loves us.

Thank you for the Bible, Lord Jesus. May we read it and learn all about you. Amen.

CELEBRATIONS

Thank you for the fun of birthdays. Thank you for my birthday today. Thank you for all the presents and all the people fussing over me. Thank you for all my family and friends who have helped make today a special day. On days like today, when I am the center of attention, help me not to forget that you are still the most important thing in my life. I like birthdays, but I want to like you even more. Amen.

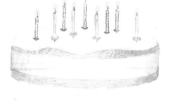

Thank you for the wedding today. Thank you for the church service and the special meal afterwards. And thank you for the delicious wedding cake. Please help the bride and bridegroom to have a happy life together. Amen.

On this Mother's Day, Lord Jesus, I thank you for my mother. Thank you for her goodness and kindness in looking after me. Thank you for her help to me as I am growing up. And I thank you, Lord Jesus, that you have been looking after us both. Amen.

Summer

Thank you for sunny days. Thank you for days when the sun is shining brightly, the sky is clear and blue, and there are no clouds in sight. Thank you that your love shines on us all, just like the sun. Amen.

Dear Jesus, please keep us safe on this trip. Please protect us as we travel, and let us arrive safely at our destination. Amen.

Father God, thank you for vacations:
for the excitement of preparing and packing,
for interesting places to explore, for new people
to meet. Give rest to those who are tired or overworked
and are not able to have a vacation away from home.
Help us to use our vacations to make new friends
and to learn new things. Amen

Dear Jesus, thank you for this time off school for us to rest and
play and spend time at home. Help us to spend some of
our time helping around the house and to be thoughtful and kind.
Amen.

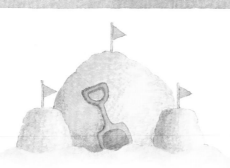

Thank you for the beach, for sand and sandcastles,
and the waves that splash my feet.
Thank you for the fun of being at the beach.
Thank you for puppet shows, and state fairs.
I like being on vacation. Amen.

Thank you, Jesus, it's great to be off school for the summer!
Thanks for all the fun things I can do when I am not at school,
for my friends and toys, and all the time that I have to play.
Help me to be friends with everybody, not just with my
favorites. And, please help me not to be a pest at home.
Amen.

Thank you, dear Jesus, for my vacation.
Thank you for the fun of being in a different city,
sleeping in a different bedroom and meeting new people.
Thank you for giving us a safe trip here.
Please look after us on our vacation. Amen.

Dear Father God,
Thank you for sea and sand,
for rocks and cliffs,
for pools and pebbles,
for shells and swimming,
for paddling and picnics.
I love the spray and the foam,
the waves
and the splash.
Thank you for all the fun of the beach. Amen.

MY WORLD

Dear God, thank you for making the world.
It is like a giant picture book – full of different
shapes and colors. Thank you for all the
amazing things in it, like trees and flowers, hills
and streams, the moon and the sun. Thank you
for the weather and thank you for all the
different kinds of animals. Thank you, God, for
making it all. Amen.

Dear Jesus, today I heard someone from another
country speaking in a different language. It
sounded very strange! He didn't speak with the
same words that I use, so I couldn't understand
what he was saying. Thank you for all the
different kinds of people. Amen.

Lord, you have given us water: clean, pure and fit to drink, and we poison the rivers with chemicals and dirt. Lord, you have made the world, help us to care for it.

Lord, you have made the wind, the air that we breathe, which gives us life, and we fill the air with fumes from our factories and cars. Lord, you have made the world, help us to care for it.

Lord, forgive us and help us to see how we can live in your world, without spoiling it for ourselves and others. Amen.

Dear Father, we love all the beautiful things you have made. May we never spoil or neglect them. Father, show us how to be kind to all your creatures, so that we may help you to take care of them. Amen.

Dear Jesus, why do people put garbage and
pollution into the rivers and reservoirs?
Forgive us for doing this. Please help us not
to spoil water or to waste it. Teach us to be
careful so that we can look after your world.
Amen.

Thank you for the water. It is so important. It makes the crops
grow so that the farmers can harvest the food we eat. It comes
out of our taps for us to use for cooking, drinking and washing.
Thank you for the oceans, and for lakes and rivers. Thank you
for all the different kinds of plants that grow there, and for the
animals and insects that live there. I like throwing in stones and
making them skim along the surface. Amen.

Dear Jesus, thank you for big things
and little things; from the highest
mountain to a single blade of grass;
for the wide, wide sky and the
deepest ocean. All these things you
have given us. We must look after
them. Help us to remember that
you are interested in everything no
matter how big or small it might be.
Amen.

THE UNIVERSE

Dear Lord, thank you for the sun.
Thank you for the light and the heat
it gives to make the trees and plants
grow. Thank you for its warmth
and brightness on hot sunny days.
Thank you for the beautiful sunsets
we sometimes see on the horizon.
Amen.

When I look up at the sky at night, it is difficult for me to
understand that you are out there, and that you created all that
I can see. It is hard for me to understand that it was you who
made the sun shine so brightly, and who put the stars and
planets in their places. Thank you for all the things you have
made, dear Jesus, and help me to understand you and your
world more. Amen.

Dear Jesus, I saw a program about space on TV today. They showed pictures of all the rockets and spaceships that fly out for millions of miles into space. They said that in the future there will be people living on the moon.

I'd like to go into space. I'd like to fly in a spaceship and visit all the moons and planets. It must be great in space. Thank you for making space great, Jesus. Amen.

Dear God, it must have been very exciting when you were making all the stars and planets in the universe. At night time I can see the stars you made shining in space, millions of miles away. Thank you because, even though space is so big, you still care for us here on tiny planet earth. Amen.

APOLOGIZING

I'm sorry when I'm unkind
and when I forget to say thank you.
I'm sorry when I don't take care of my toys
or when I don't want to share them.
I'm sorry for sometimes being naughty
and then pretending it wasn't me.
I'm sorry for not being careful
and for sulking at bedtime. Amen.

Marjorie Newman

Lord Jesus, I know there are some things which are wrong.
I know this because the Bible tells me so. Things like telling
lies, cheating, stealing, saying bad things about people, and
not helping others when I can. Help me to be a good person,
and always to say I'm sorry when I have done something
wrong. Amen.

Dear Jesus, it is very hard to be good. Even though I try,
I can't seem to stop saying and doing all kinds of things
that I shouldn't. Even when I say nice things sometimes,
I am still thinking cruel and nasty things inside. I'm sorry, Lord.
Please help me to be a better person. Amen.

Lord, I'm sorry for the times when I'm not helpful:
I leave my clothes and toys all over the floor;
I forget to take off my muddy boots and shoes;
I spill my drinks and paints on the furniture;
I make noise when other people want me to be quiet.
Lord, please make me more helpful every day. Amen.

Geoffrey Marshall-Taylor

Dear Jesus, I did something I was told not to do
when nobody was looking. I'm sorry. Please don't
let me think that I can do bad things just because
other people cannot see me, because I know that
you can see me wherever I am. Amen.

GRACES

A large crowd gathered to hear Jesus speak about the kingdom of God. More than five thousand people had gathered and when the sun began to set at the end of the day, the disciples said to Jesus, "Send the people away so that they can go to the villages and farms round here and find food and lodging, because this is a lonely place." But Jesus said to them, "You give them something to eat!" The disciples answered, "All we have are five loaves and two fish." Jesus said, "Then bring them here to me." He ordered the people to sit down in groups of about fifty. Then Jesus took the loaves and the fish and, looking up to heaven, He thanked God for them, broke them, and gave them to the disciples to give out among the people. And all the people ate and had enough.

Based on Matthew 14

Dear Jesus, help us to be thankful that we have plenty to eat in this country. Help us to remember all those people in other countries who have to go to bed hungry. Amen.

For food to eat and those who prepare it;
For health to enjoy it and friends to share it;
Thank you, Heavenly Father. Amen.

Traditional

Dear God, thank you for looking
after us. Thank you for this food
and drink. Please may we be
always thankful. Amen.

Now my plate is full
But soon it will be gone
Thank you for my food
And please help those with none. Amen.

PRAYERS FOR HELP

Lord, when we are afraid, you are with us, just like our mothers and fathers who hold our hands when we are in the dark or in a strange place. Although we cannot see you, we know that you promise always to be near us. Thank you, Lord. Amen.

Dear Lord, it is so silly to be sitting in a room and suddenly feel that every eye is on you. To feel sudden warmth. To know that your face is changing color. To pretend to sneeze to hide it. To hear some unfeeling person say, "Ha! Ha! She's blushing."

It's so silly, but so unpleasant. Dear, understanding Father, in your loving kindness, you can feel with us when all we want to do is run from the room and hide. Help us not to hide, but grow in confidence, ready to look all men in the eye as we do your will. Amen.

Please look after my family today
and be with me as I play with my friends.
Please help children who are hungry
and grownups who can't find a job.
Please take care of people who are sick
and be with those who are lonely.
Please teach me to care for your world,
your animals, plants and trees.
Please remind me of your love – all the time. Amen.

Marjorie Newman

Dear Jesus, I have had an argument with my friend
and we have stopped talking to each other.
I don't want it to be this way.
Please help me to be brave so that I can say I'm sorry
and make us friends again. Amen.

Dear God, you are wise and loving,
You are great and strong;
Glad when we do right,
Grieved when we do wrong.

Father God, my Father,
Guide me every hour;
Keep me safe and shield me
From temptation's power. Amen.

Traditional (adapted)

Dear Jesus, sometimes I find it
difficult being a friend of yours.
The other children make fun of
me and call me names.
Dear Jesus, please help me not to
join in when the other children are
being bad. I want to be friends with
them, Lord Jesus, but I want to be
your friend even more. Amen.

Dear Jesus, my mommy and daddy have just had a bad argument, and I feel like crying. I don't like it when they are angry with each other. Please help them to be friends and please help us to be a happy family again. Amen.

Dear Jesus, please help me.
I keep getting bullied at school.
I don't know why they do it
and I'm scared, but I know I must
tell the teacher.
Please make it so that we can
all be friends. Amen.

Dear Jesus, at school I often feel very shy. I get embarrassed when the teacher asks me to say something for the rest of the class to hear, and my face goes red. Please help me be more confident. Amen.

HEAVEN

Dear Jesus, I feel very sad.
My grandma has died,
and I don't know what to think.
I'm going to miss her.
I know that when people die,
they can go to live
with you forever.
Please make it so
that when I die
I can live with you forever.
Amen.

Jesus appeared to His disciples on many occasions after His resurrection, telling them many things. On the last occasion, as He was blessing them, He was taken up into heaven before their very eyes, and a cloud hid Him from their sight. While the disciples were looking up into the sky at Jesus, two men dressed all in white stood beside them. "Why do you stand here looking into the sky? This same Jesus, who has been taken from you into heaven, will come back in the same way you have seen Him go." And the disciples worshipped Jesus.

Based on Luke 24; Acts 1

Lord Jesus, the disciples must have been very sad when you left them to go back up into heaven. But we know from the Bible that you did not leave us.
Though you are in heaven, you are still watching over us, and still waiting for us to look to you. Thank you that although you are no longer on this earth, you have not forgotten about us, and you are still waiting to help us when we ask you. Amen.

Dear Jesus, thank you for heaven.
It's going to be great and it will
never end. Thank you that we will
be able to live with you forever.
Thank you that when people we
love die they go to live with you
forever. Amen.

GOODNIGHT

Goodnight, Jesus. It has been a busy
day and I am exhausted. Please help
me and my family to sleep well.
Amen.

Now we go to sleep,
keep us safe we pray. Amen.

Jesus, tender Shepherd, hear me;
Bless your little lamb tonight;
Through the darkness please be near me;
Watch my sleep till morning light.

All this day your hand has led me,
And I thank you for your care;
You have clothed me, warmed and fed me;
Listen to my evening prayer.

Let my sins be all forgiven;
Bless the friends I love so well;
Take me, when I die, to heaven,
Happy there with you to dwell. Amen.

Mary Lundie Duncan, 1814–1840 (adapted)

INDEX OF FIRST LINES

ACKNOWLEDGMENTS

The publishers would like to thank all those who have contributed prayers to this anthology. Prayers not otherwise credited were written by Mike Brooks.

CELEBRATION/THANKYOU MUSIC: *If I were a butterfly* by Brian Howard p28 copyright © 1974, 1975 Celebration/Thankyou Music, PO Box 75, Eastbourne, East Sussex, BN23 6NW.
CHURCH MISSIONARY SOCIETY: *Lord of the loving heart* p55 first published in 1933 by the Church Missionary Society.
HARPERCOLLINS: *O, God, bless and help all those who have to face life* p37 from *More Prayers for Young People* © 1977 by William Barclay, published by Fount paperbacks.
Animals in zoos, in films, in books p38; *Dear God, you know all about me* p52 and *Lord, I'm sorry for the times when I'm not helpful* p83 from *Let's Pray Together* © 1981 Geoffrey Marshall-Taylor, published by Collins.
Thanks for the rabbit by Tony Davies p52 from *Please God* © 1989 BBC Radio Leicester, published by Fount paperbacks.
HUNT & THORPE: *I'm sorry when I'm unkind* p82 and *Please look after my family today* p87 by Marjorie Newman, © Hunt & Thorpe.
THE NATIONAL CHRISTIAN EDUCATION COUNCIL:
Dear God, we wake in the morning p31; *Dear Lord, when the winter winds howl round the house* p40; *Lord Jesus, you lived at Nazareth, Home is the place we come to* and *God, our Father, please help all the people in the world* p41; *Mothers and fathers are the people* p44; *Lord, we are glad we have brothers and sisters* p45; *Lord Jesus, you told us to love* p54 and *Lord, when we are afraid* p86 from *When You Pray With 3–6s.*
The end of school brings a sense of release p15; *Lord, we thank you that when you filled the world* p32; *Lord, often we say 'I'm hungry'* p33; *Lord God, when you made us* p34; *Jesus, you knew that you needed friends* p35; *Lord Jesus, you know what it is like to be sad* p60; *Lord God, Lord of the world* p61; *God our Father, we thank you that the Bible* p68; *Father God, thank you for vacations* p73 and *Lord, you have given us water* p77 from *When You Pray With 7–10s.*
Dear Lord, it is so silly p86 from *When You Pray With Young People.*
Dear Father God, thank you for sea and sand p75 from *Prayers to use with Young People.*
First the seed by Lilian Cox p13 and *We thank you loving Father God* by Hilda Rostron p30 from *New Child Songs.* All publications © National Christian Education Council.
THE NATIONAL SOCIETY: *We praise God for things we see* by Maria Matilda Penstone p26 © The National Society (Church of England) for Promoting Religious Education.
THE SOCIETY FOR PROMOTING CHRISTIAN KNOWLEDGE: *Autumn Days* p10 is taken from *Good and Gay* by Mary Osborn and is reproduced by kind permission of SPCK (London).
WORLD INTERNATIONAL PUBLISHING LTD: *My tongue can taste all sorts of things* by Marjorie Newman p37 from *My Book of Prayers.*